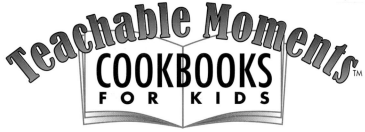

Teachable Moments
COOKBOOKS
FOR KIDS ™

Party Time!

Brenda C. Ward
Jane Cabaniss Jarrell

WORD
Kids!®

WORD PUBLISHING
Dallas·London·Vancouver·Melbourne

Photography   Donald Fuller

Design   Sabra Smith

Managing Editor   Laura Minchew

Project Manager   Beverly Phillips

Food Styling   Jane Jarrell

Teachable Moments Cookbooks for Kids
Party Time!

LIBRARY OF CONGRESS CATALOGING-IN-PUBLICATION DATA

Ward, Brenda.
    Party time! / Brenda C. Ward, Jane Cabaniss Jarrell.
      p.   cm.—(Teachable moments cookbooks for kids)
    ISBN 0–8499–3673–X
    1. Cookery. 2. Children's parties I. Jarrell, Jane Cabaniss.
    1961– . II. Title. III. Series.
    TX714.W268   1995
    641.5'123—dc20   95–11648
                                                      CIP

Printed in the United States of America
95 96 97 98 99   R R D   9 8 7 6 5 4 3 2 1

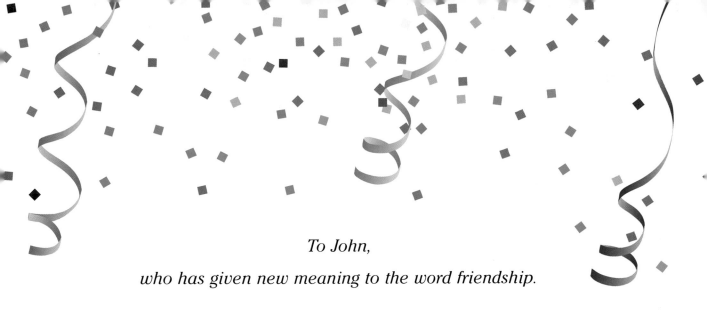

To John,
who has given new meaning to the word friendship.

B.C.W.

To my parents, Bill and Sarah Cabaniss.
As a loving team, they instilled in me a foundation of values that
will remain true always.

J.C.J.

Contents

How to Use This Book 6

Friendship 9
"Make a New Friend" Party 10
Alphabet Pound Cake
Colored Powdered Sugar
"Friendship Grows" Party 12
Friendship Bread Starter
Friendship Bread
Fruit-Flavored Glaze
Fruit and Berry Butters (Raspberry, Orange, Blueberry)
"Happy Good-bye" Party 16
Confetti Brownies
Chocolate Icing
"Faraway Friend" Party 20
Texas-Shaped Nachos
Family Pen-Pal Party 22
Candy Star Cutouts
All-Night Party 24
Wake-Up Waffle Sandwiches
Cocoa Supreme

Cooperation 26
"Working Together" Pizza Party 26
Mini Bagel Pizza Bites
English Muffin Pizzas
Dessert Pizza Trio (Funny Face, Pinwheel, Four-Fruit)
"Teamwork" Practice Party 30
Power Punch
Power Popcorn
Neighborhood "Stone Soup" Party 32
Stone Soup with Cornbread Stars
"Fun Family Salad" Party 34
Sam and Sally Salad

Respect for All People 36
Gingerbread People Painting Party 38
Gingerbread People
Royal Icing
Piñata Party 40
Tortillas
Fiesta Guacamole
Refried Beans
Oriental Tea Party 44
Fortune Cookies
Flavored Colored Sugars (Strawberry, Lemon, Mint)
"Happy Hanukkah" Party 48
Latkes
Homemade Applesauce

Serving Others 68

Food Bank Party 69

Lollipop Cookies
Fruited Sugar Icing

Nursing Home Party 72

Peanut Butter and Jelly Bars

"Toys for Tots" Party 74

Mom's Christmas Wreaths

Fun Fudge Party 76

Peppermint Fudge

**Appreciation for Creation
52**

**Johnny Appleseed
Tree-Planting Party 53**

"Mr. Cat" Chocolate Apple
Striped Chocolate Apple
Sprinkled Apple

Recycling Party 58

Main Course Trash
Healthy Trash
Dessert Trash

Zoo Party 62

Backpack Bundle Sandwiches
*(Monkey Face, Elephant-
Shaped Tortilla)*
Monkey Chow
*Chocolate-Dipped Animal
Crackers*

Family Clean-Up Party 66

Cookout Banana Splits

How to Use This Book
A Guide for Parents

Face it—parenting is hectic. Add the responsibility of teaching our children all the values and principles that we as parents want to pass on, and you've gone from hectic to one huge guilt trip! Exactly when—between soccer, birthday parties, ballet, and softball—is there time to teach our children all the priceless principles they will need to hold in life?

The *Teachable Moments Cookbooks for Kids* are designed to help solve this problem by providing children and parents with natural teaching and learning times through an activity that children love—cooking! Teachers have known for years that cooking is a wonderful vehicle for teaching. It reinforces math and language skills, and it encourages organization and sequential thinking. Best of all, it is a fun learning experience for children.

To make the most of the recipes and activities in this book, try the following helpful suggestions:

Have a PLAN:

🍎 Decide what value you would like to cover with your children and look under that particular section in the book. Check the parties in that section to find the one that best fits your needs.

🍎 Read the suggested recipe to determine how many children are appropriate for that particular activity. If inviting more than four to five children, consider asking one of their parents to come along and help.

🍎 Plan ahead on the family parties, too. Pick a time of the week that is the least busy and stressful for everyone. Plan on a relaxing, fun time.

🍎 Check recipes to make sure you've allotted enough preparation time. Some steps may need to be done the day before in order to finish the recipes in the length of time you have (for example, cookie dough that needs to chill for several hours).

Don't forget to PREPARE:

🍴 Use the **Things you'll need** box *(see example on right)* and **Ingredients** section as easy references for setting up cooking trays ahead of time. Allow the children to pour, measure, and chop, but have all ingredients and equipment set up ahead of time.

🍴 Advance preparation that needs to be done by you, such as browning meat or chopping onions, should be done ahead of time.

🍴 Prepare a safe cooking environment for the children. Seated around a large table works great, but seated on a stool next to the stove is dangerous! Many schools use individual heating units in their cooking activities, and you may find that one would be well worth the investment. For best results, plug the cord in on the side of the table where you are sitting, and have the children work opposite you.

🍴 Discuss rules for safety and sanitation before you begin any part of the activity, while you still have the children's total attention!

Things you'll need:

⚬═ wooden spoon
◣▬ knife
◤ cutting board

Sample: "Things you'll need" box

Remember the PURPOSE:

🥄 Read or have children read the text as you begin each activity.

🥄 Check the **Teachable Moments** box *(see example to the left)* that is included for each activity to give you suggestions on how to make the most out of each one. Read the box ahead of time and remember the objective of each activity as you do it with the children.

🥄 Sure, it's easier to prepare these foods yourself, but don't forget the long-term goal—you are passing on critical values to your children.

Teachable Moments

While making this recipe, talk with the children about feelings. You might play a guessing game and try to guess what each child is feeling. Reinforce that it's important to share our feelings with others because it helps us understand each other. For example, a child who feels sad about a friend moving away will probably feel better when he knows that others feel sad, too.

 Teachable Moments information box

Sample of a value teaching from one of the cooking activities.

What is a friend? A friend is someone who makes you feel special. He or she might laugh at your jokes, or enjoy the same kind of books. You may both like to wear jeans to school on the same day, or you may enjoy spending the night together on the weekends. You care about each other, and you treat each other with kindness and respect. This special relationship that you have with someone you care about is called a

Friendship

Friendships are not all the same. You have many different kinds of friends. Some friends you see every day at school, and others may live far away so that you don't get to see them as often. Some friends you know really well, and others you may be just getting to know. Having different types of friendships is great. You will have many friends throughout your life, and each one will be special in his or her own way. 　　　An important rule to remember about friendship is that **having** a good friend means **being** a good friend. The Golden Rule says it this way: "Do for other people as you want them to do for you." If you can remember this rule—to treat others the way you want to be treated—then all the rest should work out just fine! Having parties with friends is one of the enjoyable things you can do together. This section shows you some recipes that can add to the fun of parties with your friends.

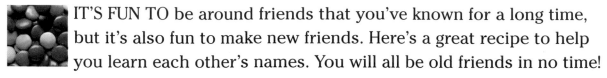

"Make a New Friend" Party

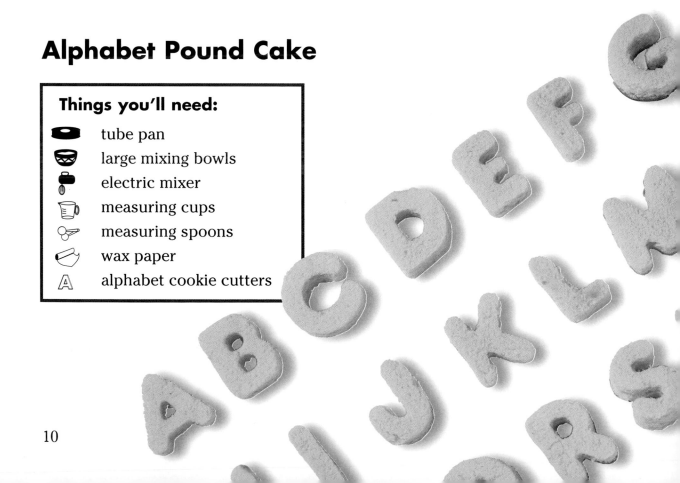

IT'S FUN TO be around friends that you've known for a long time, but it's also fun to make new friends. Here's a great recipe to help you learn each other's names. You will all be old friends in no time!

Step 1: For this party, find two or three kids who are new in your neighborhood, church, or school. Invite them over with two or three friends that you already know.

Step 2: If you have a few hours, let everyone help prepare the alphabet pound cake and colored powdered sugar. If you don't have much time, make the pound cake ahead of time or use a store-bought pound cake.

Step 3: Write everyone's names on pieces of paper, and put all the names in a bowl. Have each child draw a name out of the bowl and cut out and decorate that name. Take a picture and eat!

Alphabet Pound Cake

Things you'll need:

- tube pan
- large mixing bowls
- electric mixer
- measuring cups
- measuring spoons
- wax paper
- alphabet cookie cutters

Alphabet Pound Cake

Ingredients:

3 cups sugar
1 1/4 cups butter, softened
6 eggs
2 teaspoons vanilla extract
1/2 teaspoon almond extract
3 cups all-purpose flour
1 teaspoon baking powder
1/4 teaspoon salt
1 cup whole milk

1. Preheat oven to 350 degrees.
2. Grease and flour tube pan.
3. Beat sugar, butter, eggs, vanilla extract, and almond extract in a large mixing bowl until well blended.
4. Mix flour, baking powder, and salt in another bowl. Add into egg mixture alternately with milk on low speed. Pour batter into tube pan.
5. Bake until a wooden pick inserted in the center comes out clean (approximately 1 hour and 15 minutes).
6. Cool and remove from pan.
7. Cut 3/4–inch thick slices and lay out on wax paper.
8. With alphabet cookie cutters, cut out letters to spell each name.
9. Decorate with colored powdered sugar and sprinkles.

Makes 1 cake. Slices enough for approximately 24 letters.

Colored Powdered Sugar

Things you'll need:

 sifter
 measuring cup
 measuring spoons
 sugar shaker
bowl

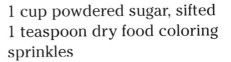

Ingredients:

1 cup powdered sugar, sifted
1 teaspoon dry food coloring
sprinkles

1. In a medium-sized bowl, sift the dry coloring and powdered sugar together. You may need to do this several times.
2. Put the colored powdered sugar into a clean sugar shaker. Shake it onto your alphabet cake cutouts.
3. Top with sprinkles.

Teachable Moments

Children learn best by following your example. Inviting one of the new children's parents over for coffee during the party would reinforce this lesson tremendously.

"Friendship Grows" Party

 HERE'S A GREAT party idea to kick off the summer, or just for something fun to do during the school year!

Step 1: Make a batch of Friendship Bread Starter at least ten days before your party. You will have enough starter to share with three friends. Write each recipe—the starter recipe, bread and icing recipe, and butter recipes—on an 8" x 10" sheet of paper. Make photocopies of each for your three friends.

Step 2: After your three friends arrive, start by painting your own handprint aprons. (Plain aprons in many colors can be found at large craft stores.) Each friend can make one set of handprints on each apron. After the handprints are finished, splatter-paint the whole apron and three fold-over recipe cards for each person. Glue the photocopies of the three recipes inside the cards.

Step 3: Then make this wonderful friendship bread and raspberry, blueberry, and orange butters.

Step 4: Have each friend take some starter home to make his own recipe of friendship bread. Each can grow enough starter to share with three friends, and so on and so on. Just like the starter, friendship grows and grows!

Teachable Moments

While you are making the bread, remind the children that they will have enough "starter" to share with three other friends, and those three friends can share it with three friends. See how many friends each of the children can name, and talk about the happiness that friends bring.

Friendship Bread Starter

The first ingredient you need for your Friendship Bread is starter. Starter is a culture you use when making certain types of bread. Without the starter, the bread wouldn't rise. It would look more like a big, flat cracker!

In a large non-metallic container combine:

2 cups milk
2 cups flour
1 cup sugar
1 package dry yeast

1. Cover loosely and let stand overnight in a warm place.
2. Stir the next day and cover loosely and refrigerate.
3. Leave in refrigerator and stir once a day for the next four days.
4. On the fifth day add:

1 cup milk
1 cup flour
1 cup sugar

5. Let stand one day in a warm place, loosely covered.
6. Refrigerate and stir every day for the next five days.
7. On the tenth day you are ready to make your bread.

Makes enough starter to make your bread and share 1 cup each with three friends.

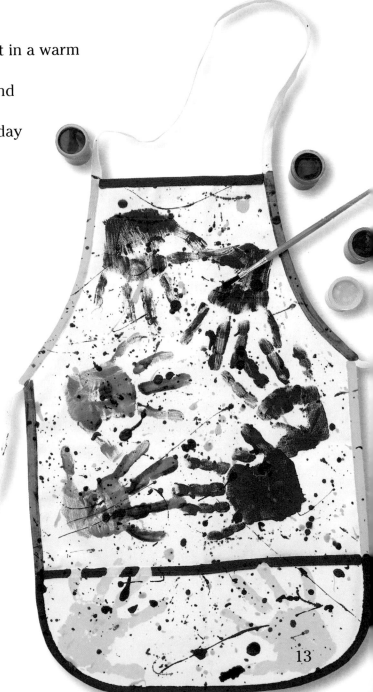

Friendship Bread

Things you'll need:

 large non-metallic mixing bowl

 measuring cups

 electric mixer

 bundt pan or muffin pan

 spoon

 3 small non-metallic bowls for starter

Ingredients:

1 cup starter
2/3 cup oil
2 tablespoons vanilla extract
1 cup sugar
3 eggs
2 cups all-purpose or bread flour
1 1/2 teaspoons salt
2 teaspoons baking powder
1 1/2 teaspoons cinnamon
1 cup fruit or
3 tablespoons brown sugar mixed with 3 teaspoons cinnamon

1. Preheat oven to 350 degrees.
2. Grease and flour bundt pan or muffin pan.
3. In the large non-metallic mixing bowl combine oil, vanilla extract, and sugar and mix well.
4. Add eggs, one at a time, and mix well.
5. Add flour, salt, baking powder, and cinnamon; stir to combine.
6. If making a fruited bread, fold in desired fruit.
7. If making brown sugar/cinnamon bread, mix sugar and cinnamon together. Pour half of the batter into a prepared pan and sprinkle the batter with the sugar mixture. Swirl with a spoon. Add the other half of the batter.
8. Bake at 350 degrees: bundt pan—40–45 minutes; muffin pan—20 minutes.

Makes 1 bundt pan or 12 muffins.

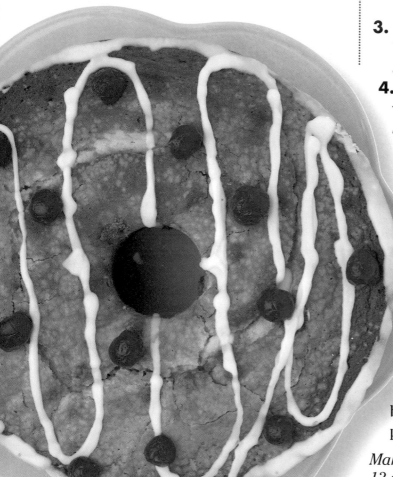

Fruit-Flavored Glaze

Ingredients:

1 cup powdered sugar, sifted
1 to 2 tablespoons fruit juice
desired color

1. Mix icing ingredients until smooth.
2. Spread or drizzle over cooled bread or muffins.
3. Garnish with fruit.

Fruit and Berry Butters

Raspberry Butter

Things you'll need:

 bowl
 wooden spoon
 knife
cutting board

Ingredients:

$1/4$ pound butter (1 stick)
$1/4$ cup raspberry preserves
1 tablespoon fresh raspberries, finely chopped

1. Soften butter to room temperature.
2. Stir until smooth and creamy.
3. Add preserves and mix well.
4. Add raspberries and mix thoroughly.
5. Refrigerate until ready to serve.

Blueberry, Raspberry, and Orange Butters

Orange Butter

Things you'll need:

 bowl
 wooden spoon
 grater (fine grade)

Ingredients:

$1/4$ pound butter (1 stick)
$1/4$ cup orange marmalade
1 teaspoon orange rind, grated

1. Soften butter to room temperature.
2. Stir until smooth and creamy.
3. Add marmalade and mix well.
4. Add grated orange rind and mix thoroughly.
5. Refrigerate until ready to serve.

Blueberry Butter

Things you'll need:

 bowl
 wooden spoon
 knife
cutting board

Ingredients:

$1/4$ pound butter (1 stick)
$1/4$ cup blueberry preserves
1 tablespoon fresh blueberries chopped

1. Soften butter to room temperature.
2. Stir until smooth and creamy.
3. Add preserves and mix well.
4. Add fresh blueberries and mix thoroughly.
5. Refrigerate until ready to serve.

Each recipe makes $1/2$ cup.

"Happy Good-bye" Party

WHEN YOU HAVE a good friend, you have many happy times together. But you may have some sad times, too, especially if one of you moves away. This is hard for both the person who is leaving and the person who is staying. If you are the friend who isn't moving, it's important to remember that if you feel sad, then your friend who is moving probably feels even worse. He will be moving to a new neighborhood and will have to go to a different school and make new friends. Everything may seem different and strange to him for a while. He may feel a little worried and afraid.

This would be a great time to plan a good-bye party to cheer up your friend—and yourself! He will feel much better about leaving if he knows how much everyone cares about him, how much he'll be missed, and how special he is to all of you. Knowing that he has good friends "back home" will make him feel better when those lonely days come after he's moved. And that's the best present that you can send with him—your friendship!

Step 1: Invite everyone to come to the party thirty minutes earlier than the honored guest. Ask each person to bring one of the ingredients for the Friendship Basket, one small package of his favorite candy, or a package of stickers or gum, and a small photo of himself to use in making an address book.

Step 2: You provide the basket, the address book, and the ingredients for the Confetti Brownies.

Teachable Moments

While making this recipe, talk with the children about feelings. You might play a guessing game and try to guess what each child is feeling. Reinforce that it's important to share our feelings with others because it helps us understand each other. For example, a child who feels sad about a friend moving away will probably feel better when he knows that others feel sad, too.

Step 3: With the colored pencils for the basket, have each child write his name, address, and phone number inside the address book. He can then glue his photo beside his name and write a short good-bye message or draw a small picture underneath.

Step 4: Before the honored guest arrives, gather all the contents together for the Friendship Basket.

- 1 large basket
- 2 bunches colored shredded paper
- 1 address book with addresses and pictures
- 1 set colored pencils
- 1 package stationery
- 1 recipe of Confetti Brownies
- 1 package of favorite candy, stickers, or gum from each child

As you make the brownies, you might share funny memories of your time together.

After the honored guest arrives, make this double recipe of Confetti Brownies together. Let the group eat half the brownies, and wrap the other half to put in the Friendship Basket. Place all the contents in the basket, wrap the basket in plastic wrap, and tie the top in a large knot. Present this cheerful basket to your honored guest at the end of the party.

Confetti Brownies

Things you'll need:

 saucepan

 spoon

 measuring cups

 measuring spoons

 baking dish (13" x 9")

Ingredients:

2 squares (2 ounces) unsweetened chocolate
2/3 cup shortening
2 cups sugar
4 eggs, lightly beaten
2 teaspoons vanilla extract
1 1/2 cups flour
1 teaspoon baking powder
1 teaspoon salt

1. Preheat oven to 350 degrees.
2. In a saucepan, heat chocolate and shortening over low heat, stirring constantly until melted.
3. Remove from heat and stir in sugar, eggs, and vanilla extract.
4. Stir in remaining ingredients and pour into a greased 13" x 9" baking dish. Bake for 25 minutes or until wooden pick inserted in center comes out clean.

Makes 12 to 15 servings.

Chocolate Icing

Things you'll need:

 microwave-safe bowl

 spoon

 measuring cup

 measuring spoons

Ingredients:

2 cups milk chocolate morsels
4 tablespoons cream
2 teaspoons vanilla extract

1. Place ingredients in a microwave-safe bowl and microwave on medium power in 40-second intervals, stirring between intervals until melted.
2. Pour over prepared brownies.
3. Cover with your choice of confetti.

Confetti

Ingredients:

chocolate candies
gumdrops
sprinkles
gummy bears
jelly beans

Sprinkle any of these ingredients liberally over brownies.

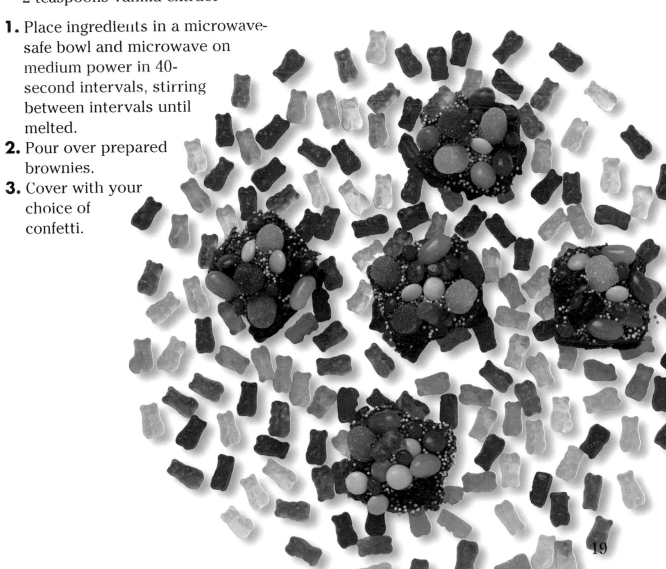

"Faraway Friend" Party

 MANY OF YOUR friends live in the same neighborhood or town you live in, and you see them often at church or school. Other friends may live in another city or state, and you don't get to spend much time together.

Even if you aren't able to see each other all the time, you can still have fun with friends who live far away. And you can do something special with them that you don't get to do with friends who live nearby—you can send letters and packages to each other in the mail! Also, writing back and forth to a friend in another place is fun because you learn about the state or country in which she lives. And she can learn about the place where you live, too.

If you have a friend who has moved to another state, here's a great party idea to help you keep in touch with each other and learn about the new place in which she lives. Keeping in touch with her will be even more fun if you invite some of your friends who know her to a fun "faraway friend" party.

Step 1: Think about the state in which you live. What is special about your state? Does it have a unique shape? Or a beautiful state bird or flower? What is a popular food to eat in your state? Use these answers as a guide in planning your party.

Step 2: You can make cute stationery using the shape of your state or your state bird or flower. You might sponge-paint, make paint prints with cookie cutters, or use stencils and markers to

Teachable Moments

If your child has recently had a friend move and has made the transition a little too easily, this might be a good time to remind her that having a good friend means being a good friend. Keeping in touch with a friend who's moved can mean a lot to someone who may not have had time to make new friends yet.

make your stationery. Just be creative! Have each person write a short note to the faraway friend.

Step 3: Together, make a favorite state recipe. If you can, make the recipe and send it in a box with your letters. (Be sure to make enough to eat some now!) If your chosen recipe can't be mailed, write the recipe down on a decorated recipe card and include it with your letters. If some of the ingredients for the recipe can be mailed, then send those along with the recipe. You can still make the recipe together and take a photo of everyone around the recipe.

Step 4: In your letters, tell your friend that you'd like to learn more about her new state. Maybe she'll have a "faraway friend" party, too!

A favorite recipe from our state of Texas is nachos. Nachos are very popular in Texas, and we added a sweet-pepper star to mark our city of Dallas. We weren't able to mail our recipe, but we could mail Texas-shaped chips and salsa.

The state flower of Texas is the bluebonnet, so we made finger-painted bluebonnets on our stationery and included bluebonnet seeds in our package.

Texas-Shaped Nachos

Things you'll need:

 microwave-safe plate

 grater

 measuring cup

★ star cutter

knife

cutting board

Ingredients:

1 package Texas-shaped tortilla chips

1 cup cheddar cheese, grated

1 small red bell pepper, cut into star shapes

1 small can black olives, sliced

1. Spread out tortilla chips in a single layer on a microwave-safe plate.
2. Sprinkle with grated cheese.
3. Place in a microwave oven for one minute on medium power until cheese melts.
4. Sprinkle with black olives and red pepper stars.

Makes 4 servings.

Family Pen-Pal Party

IT'S FUN WRITING letters to a friend who has moved away. But did you know that you can write letters to someone you've never met who lives far away? When you exchange letters with someone you've never met who lives in another state or country, that person is called a pen pal.

There are many different types of pen-pal programs. Your mom or dad can help you find one. Most local libraries have information on pen-pal programs, and many churches and schools can help pair you with a pen pal.

If your pen pal is in another country, you will want to send something with your letters that tells him about the country you live in—the United States of America. Here's a neat recipe idea that should be mailable to just about anywhere in the world! Just make these cookies with your family, put them in a large, sealable plastic bag, and wrap the bag in red, white, and blue tissue paper. You may want to include styrofoam "peanuts" in the box to protect your cookies from breakage. Enclose a letter and a picture of your family for your pen pal. You are on your way to a fun, new friendship!

Teachable Moments

Writing to a child in another country can be an invaluable learning experience for the whole family. Your child will not only gain a better understanding of friendship but will also be exposed to new geography, foreign languages, and a different culture.

Candy Star Cutouts

Things you'll need:

- wax paper
- rolling pin
- cookie sheet
- foil
- large star-shaped cookie cutter
- small star-shaped cookie cutter
- plastic bag
- spoon

Ingredients:

1 package prepared sugar cookie dough

flour

15 red hard candies

1. On a sheet of wax paper that has been sprinkled with flour, roll out the tube of sugar cookie dough with a rolling pin to a thickness of 1/4".
2. Line a cookie sheet with foil.
3. Cut out the dough with a three-inch star-shaped cookie cutter and place stars on the foil-lined cookie sheet.
4. Use the smaller star cutter to cut out the center of each cookie. Remove the smaller star-shaped dough and save.
5. Place the hard candies in a plastic bag and crush finely with a rolling pin.
6. Spoon the crushed candies into the star-shaped center, using enough candy to cover the shape of the star cutout.
7. Bake the large cookies in a 375-degree oven for eight minutes or until cookies are golden brown. Bake the little star cookies at 375 degrees for four to five minutes or until golden brown.

Makes 3 to 4 dozen.

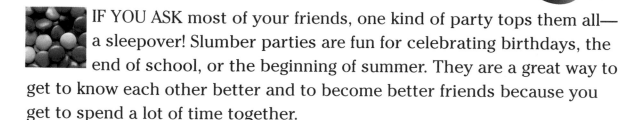

All-Night Party

IF YOU ASK most of your friends, one kind of party tops them all—a sleepover! Slumber parties are fun for celebrating birthdays, the end of school, or the beginning of summer. They are a great way to get to know each other better and to become better friends because you get to spend a lot of time together.

Here is a fantastic breakfast recipe that everyone is sure to love. Wake-Up Waffle Sandwiches and Cocoa Supreme will be the best slumber party breakfast ever! And after having your friends spend the night, preparing them will be easy on your mom and dad, too!

Step 1: Have a parent fry the bacon and heat the cocoa. You can help measure the ingredients for the cocoa.

Step 2: Toast your own waffles and make your sandwich. Then fix your own cocoa with the special condiments. After you're through eating, don't forget to clear your dishes.

Wake-Up Waffle Sandwiches

Things you'll need:

- toaster
- small bowl
- measuring spoons
- knife and spoon

Teachable Moments

Say the words "slumber party" to most parents and you create an immediate sense of dread. But slumber parties are a wonderful opportunity for children to "bond" with each other. You don't need to have a huge group—two or three children should be fine. Set reasonable and understandable rules for behavior, plan activities with your child beforehand, and you will survive!

Ingredients:

6 round frozen waffles
4 tablespoons strawberry jam
2 tablespoons cream cheese,
   softened
4 slices bacon, crisply fried and
   crumbled
fresh strawberries

1. Prepare waffles in toaster according
to package directions.
2. In a small bowl, combine jam,
cream cheese, and crumbled bacon.
3. Spread one side of a waffle with the
cream cheese/bacon mixture. Top
with fresh strawberries and the
second waffle to make a sandwich.

Makes 3 sandwiches.

Cocoa Supreme

Things you'll need:

 saucepan
 spoon
 measuring cups
 measuring spoons

Ingredients:

$1/3$ cup sugar
$1/3$ cup cocoa
$1/4$ teaspoon salt
$1/2$ cup water
5 cups milk
$1/2$ teaspoon vanilla extract
condiments

1. Mix sugar, cocoa, and salt in a two-
quart saucepan.
2. Add water and heat to
boiling, stirring constantly.
3. Simmer and stir two
minutes.
4. Stir in milk; heat
through, but do not boil.
5. Stir in vanilla extract.
6. Serve with a tray of
condiments.

Condiments:

miniature
   marshmallows
mini chocolate morsels
peppermints

Makes 5 to 6 servings.

25

 **You have probably heard** a parent or a teacher at school talk about cooperation. To cooperate means to work together for a common purpose. Cooperation can happen with friends or with your family, during work or play.

Cooperation

is a very important part of life. Just as there is a time for working on your own, there are also times for working together. Children aren't the only people who have to cooperate. Parents cooperate, too! They have to cooperate with other people at work, in car-pools, or with each other at home. Working together, helping each other, and sharing with each other—that's cooperation. Good things happen when you work together.

"Working Together" Pizza Party

Cooperation means working together, but that doesn't mean that the work isn't fun. Here's a great pizza party idea that will be so much fun you won't think it is work at all!

Invitation

Teachable Moments

The key to this party is assigning specific jobs to each child. This will enable everyone to recognize clearly that her individual part in making the pizza helped create the finished product. Talk about the fact that even though everyone had a different job to do, each job was equally important in making the pizzas.

Step 1: Make cute pizza party invitations and ask each person to bring one or two of the following ingredients. (You will be dividing into three groups, so you will need to invite at least eight children—so there will be nine including you.) You provide all the pizza crusts: the bagels, the English muffins, and the cookie dough for the dessert pizza.

Ingredients for guests to bring:

prepared pizza sauce (14 ounces)
pepperoni slices (24)
parmesan cheese ($1/4$ cup)
ground turkey ($1/2$ pound)
mild cheddar cheese (1 cup)
strawberry glaze (12 ounces)
candy corn ($1/4$ cup)
gumdrops ($1/4$ cup)
marshmallows ($1/4$ cup)
strawberries ($1/4$ cup diced plus slices)
kiwi ($1/4$ cup diced plus slices)
blueberries ($1/4$ cup plus extras)
pineapple ($1/4$ cup diced)
apple

Step 2: Divide into three groups:
> *Group 1:* makes the Mini Bagel Pizza Bites
> *Group 2:* makes the English Muffin Pizzas
> *Group 3:* makes the Dessert Pizza Trio

Step 3: Have each person in each group be responsible for doing a certain step. One person can put the sauce on, another can grate the cheese,

another can slice strawberries, and so forth.

Step 4: Have everyone eat the pizzas and see how great cooperating can be!

Mini Bagel Pizza Bites

Things you'll need:
cookie sheet
knife and spoon

Ingredients:

12 mini bagels, thawed and split
$1/2$ cup prepared pizza sauce
24 slices pepperoni
$1/4$ cup parmesan cheese, shredded

1. Place bagels on cookie sheet.
2. Spoon pizza sauce on each bagel.
3. Top each bagel with one slice of pepperoni and sprinkle with parmesan cheese.
4. Bake in a 350-degree oven for ten minutes.

Makes 12 servings.

English Muffin Pizzas

Things you'll need:

- cookie sheet
- knife and spoon
- rubber spatula
- measuring spoons
- measuring cup

Ingredients:

6 wheat English muffins, split

$3/4$ cup prepared pizza sauce

$1/2$ pound ground turkey, cooked and drained

$1/2$ teaspoon salt

$1/2$ teaspoon pepper

1 cup mild cheddar cheese, grated

1. Place English muffins on cookie sheet.

2. Spoon on prepared pizza sauce and spread to cover evenly.

3. Spoon cooked ground turkey on each muffin slice and sprinkle lightly with salt and pepper.

4. Top each muffin with grated cheese.

5. Bake in a 350-degree oven for ten minutes.

Makes 12 servings.

Dessert Pizza Trio

Things you'll need:

- wax paper
- rolling pin
- large cookie sheets (or 3 small pizza pans)
- rubber spatula
- knife and spoon
- measuring cups

Ingredients:

2 packages prepared sugar cookie dough

flour

strawberry glaze (12 ounces)

1. Roll out prepared cookie dough on a piece of wax paper sprinkled with flour.

2. Cut from the dough three large circles (each eight to ten inches in diameter).

3. Using leftover dough, form two small circles for ears for the Funny Face pizza. Place ears on the top edge of one of the circles.

4. Place cookie dough on large cookie sheets or pizza pans sprayed with cooking spray. Bake in a 350-degree oven for ten minutes or until lightly browned. Cool.

5. Spread cookies with strawberry glaze and top with the ingredients for your favorite pizza.

Makes 10 to 12 servings.

Funny Face Pizza

several blueberries
kiwi slices
strawberries for garnish
apple slices for bow tie
    and hat

Pinwheel Pizza

1/4 cup candy corn
1/4 cup gumdrops
1/4 cup marshmallows

Four-Fruit Pizza

1/4 cup pineapple, diced
1/4 cup kiwi, diced
1/4 cup strawberries, diced
1/4 cup blueberries

"Teamwork" Practice Party

WORKING TOGETHER can be fun, but so can playing together. Did you know that even playing together takes cooperation? One time when cooperation or working together is important is when playing team sports. Cooperation in sports is usually called "teamwork." Can you imagine what a game would be like if everyone decided he just wanted to do his own thing? In order to play team sports, you must have cooperation not only among the players on the same team, but also between the two teams that are playing each other.

Playing a game in team sports takes cooperation, but so does practicing for a game. Practicing alone isn't very effective. Practicing with a friend or two can improve everyone's game.

If you and a few friends need to work together and practice on a certain sport, here's a recipe to reward all of you for your hard work and cooperation!

Step 1: If you play sports on a team, invite a few friends from your team over to practice. Or, if you aren't playing on a team right now, invite some friends over to play a favorite sport.

Step 2: For a healthy energy-booster after practicing, make Power Punch and Power Popcorn. This will be a treat after working so hard!

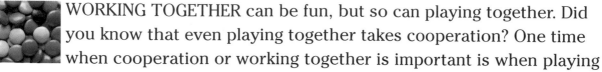

Teachable Moments

To emphasize cooperation and teamwork during the team practice, use this reverse approach. Whisper the word "cooperative" to all but one of the children—whisper "uncooperative" to him. This child is "it." Begin practice and see who can guess first which child is playing the uncooperative team member. Switch players and start the game over.

30

Power Punch

Ingredients:

1 pint fresh strawberries, stems removed

1 (8-ounce) carton vanilla yogurt

8 ice cubes

1. Combine all ingredients in blender and puree until smooth.
2. Pour into plastic cups and enjoy with Power Popcorn.

Makes 2 servings.

Power Popcorn

Ingredients:

6 cups popped popcorn

$3/4$ cup sunflower seeds, shelled

$3/4$ cup currants

$1/2$ cup golden raisins

$1/2$ cup peanut butter

1 tablespoon butter

1. Place prepared popcorn in a large bowl.
2. Add sunflower seeds, currants, and raisins to popcorn. Mix well.
3. Melt peanut butter and butter in a small saucepan over medium heat and pour over popcorn mixture.
4. Stir thoroughly to combine all ingredients.

Makes 4 to 6 servings.

Neighborhood "Stone Soup" Party

ONE OF THE BEST STORIES of cooperation and sharing is found in the old tale of "Stone Soup." You can find many versions of this old story at your local library or bookstore. One good version of the story is retold by Marcia Brown, published by Macmillan Publishing Company.

Here's a party idea that is sure to be great fun and will help everyone understand the importance of working together.

Step 1: Find the story of "Stone Soup" at your local bookstore or library.

Step 2: Find a smooth stone, wash it, and boil it in water for at least fifteen minutes.

Step 3: Invite several children from your neighborhood for a "Stone Soup" Party. Ask each child to bring one or two of the vegetables from the recipe. We have included some interesting vegetables that you may not have tried before to make the recipe more fun. You provide the meat (cooked ahead of time with the seasonings), the stewed tomatoes, the pot, and the stone.

Step 4: Have a parent or one of the children read the story of "Stone Soup" to the group.

Step 5: Make the following recipe together. Start with the stone in the pot of water. After the water boils, add the pre-cooked meat. Then have everyone take turns adding his or her ingredients to the soup. While the soup is cooking, cut a pan of cornbread into star shapes using a cookie cutter.

Teachable Moments

To personalize this activity, tell your own version of "Stone Soup" using the name of your town, each child's name, etc. Emphasize that, because each person contributed to the soup, you now have a great dinner! Cooperating together works out better for everyone.

Stone Soup

Things you'll need:

 large stew pot

 spoon

 measuring cups

 measuring spoons

 knife

 cutting board

 star cookie cutter

large bowl

Ingredients:

1 pound beef tips, cut into small cubes
1 tablespoon canola oil
2 tablespoons Worcestershire sauce
6 cups water
1 cup carrots, chopped
$1/2$ cup celery, chopped
$1/2$ cup jicama, chopped
1 cup zucchini, chopped
1 cup potato, chopped
1 cup fresh green beans, snapped
$1/2$ cup leeks, chopped
$1/2$ cup green pepper, chopped
1 (16-ounce) can stewed tomatoes
1 teaspoon salt
2 cloves garlic
cornbread mix

1. Prepare the meat before your guests arrive. In a large stew pot, sauté the beef tips in canola oil for ten minutes or until browned on all sides.

2. Add 3 cups water and Worcestershire sauce and heat to boiling.

3. Cover and simmer for two hours to tenderize the meat. Cool, then transfer to a large bowl and set aside. Wash stew pot.

4. When your guests arrive, put the clean stone and 3 cups water into the empty stew pot. Bring to a boil.

5. Add all the remaining ingredients and the meat and liquid and simmer for 30 minutes.

6. Prepare cornbread mix as directed and bake.

7. Cut cornbread into star shapes.

8. Serve soup (stone removed!) in large mugs with cornbread stars on the side or on top of the soup.

Makes 8 to 10 servings.

"Fun Family Salad" Party

 COOPERATION IS IMPORTANT at school, on your soccer team, and when playing with your friends. But one of the best places to cooperate is at home, with your family.

When you are a part of a family, you do many things together. You might play together, visit grandparents together, or go to movies together. But when you are a part of a family, you must also work together. There are meals to cook, laundry to wash, and a house to keep clean. Working together on these chores is great, because the work can be done faster and is easier to do when everyone helps.

Here's an idea to show you just how fun it can be to work together as a family.

Step 1: Choose the ingredients you want to use for your Sam and Sally Salad. You can follow the suggestions in this recipe, or you can change them to fit your family's personal tastes. Be creative and use different kinds of vegetables or fruits.

Step 2: Make one salad for each person in the family. Try having each person in the family do one thing on each salad.

Step 3: Take a photo of your salads to display on your refrigerator or to send to a grandparent who lives far away.

Teachable Moments

While you're eating your salads, talk about how nice it is when everyone in the family works together. Think of other jobs you do around the house. Try to think of creative ways to help each other and make these jobs more fun.

Sam and Sally Salad

Things you'll need:

 knife

cutting board

 vegetable cutters

Ingredients:

1 to 2 heads red cabbage
1 small head iceberg lettuce
1 yellow squash
1 carrot
1 red bell pepper
1 stalk celery
1 cup smoked turkey, shredded
commercial salad dressing
1 slice American cheese

1. Gently remove the cabbage leaves from the head, using the largest outside leaves to form a "bowl" for each family member.

2. Shred lettuce with a knife and fill the red cabbage bowls.
3. Cut the neck of the yellow squash into small rounds to form the eyes.
4. Cut the carrot into disks and use a small heart cookie cutter to form the noses.
5. Cut and seed the red bell pepper to make mouths.
6. Cut slices of celery for the eyebrows.
7. Place shaved turkey around the faces for hair.
8. Cut a bow out of the American cheese slice for each Sally.
9. Serve with your favorite commercial dressing.

Serves 4.

 **You are special.** You are one of a kind, unique. There is no one else exactly like you. It's important for you to understand how special and different you are from every other person you know, because when you understand this, you can understand how unique and special others are, too. You can respect them.

Respect for All People

means that you value them. You appreciate them and think they have worth and importance. You recognize that they are made in the image of God.

You may see ways in which others are different from you. They may have differently colored hair, skin, or eyes. Or they may speak in another language that you don't understand. They may have ideas different from yours or different ways of doing things in their family. It's important to learn about other people's ways and beliefs. Then you can understand them and recognize the ways in which you are alike and the ways in which you are different from them. Being different can be good. If we all looked exactly alike, thought alike, and talked and acted in the same way, then the world would be a boring place. Our differences are what make life more interesting, and we were created to be different from each other.

Think of the world as being a big, beautiful painting made up of many colors. The Artist could have used just one color on the painting, but He didn't. And even though one color by itself can be beautiful, a whole painting with just one color would be plain and boring. Instead, God chose to use many different colors in all shades when He created all the people in His world. Just look around…the painting is beautiful!

Gingerbread People Painting Party

 PEOPLE ARE DIFFERENT colors—and not just red, yellow, black, and white. Skin colors are beautiful shades of browns, tans, pinks, and yellows. There are many different colors of skin, and each color is beautiful. And no matter what color we are on the outside, what matters is what is on the inside.

Here's a party idea that will give you the chance to create your own colorful gingerbread people. You can use several colors on each one, or you can make each cookie in a different color. It really doesn't matter, because however you decorate them, they will all taste delicious!

Step 1: Invite some friends over to make gingerbread people and several different colors of icing.

Step 2: Using paintbrushes, paint the different colors of icing on the cookies and decorate with sprinkles.

Teachable Moments

Have all the kids at the party compare their arms and look at the color of their skin. Notice how many different shades of skin colors there are. Point out that very few people actually have the same color skin.

Gingerbread People

Things you'll need:

- large bowls
- spoon
- measuring cups
- measuring spoons
- rolling pin
- sifter
- cookie sheet
- cookie cutter
- spatula

Ingredients:

$1/4$ cup butter ($1/2$ stick), softened
$1/2$ cup brown sugar
$1/2$ cup dark molasses
3 $1/2$ cups all-purpose flour
1 teaspoon baking soda
$1/2$ teaspoon ground cloves
$1/2$ teaspoon cinnamon
2 teaspoons ginger
$1/2$ teaspoon cardamom
$1/2$ teaspoon salt
$1/4$ cup water

1. In a large bowl, beat butter and sugar until creamy.
2. Stir in molasses.
3. In a separate bowl, sift together dry ingredients.
4. Add the flour mixture to the butter mixture alternately with water.
5. On a greased surface, roll dough to $1/4$–inch thickness. Press dough firmly with desired cookie cutter.
6. With a spatula, carefully move cookie dough to a greased cookie sheet.
7. Place cookie sheet in a 350-degree oven and bake for eight to ten minutes.
8. Cool and decorate with Royal Icing and sprinkles *(see below)*.

Makes 2 dozen small gingerbread people.

Royal Icing

Things you'll need:

- measuring cup
- sifter
- bowl
- food colorings
- spoon

Ingredients:

1 cup powdered sugar, sifted
1 to 2 tablespoons fruit juice
desired colors of food coloring
sprinkles

1. Mix icing ingredients until smooth.
2. Use brushes to "paint" gingerbread people with icing.
3. Decorate with sprinkles of different sizes, creating facial features if desired.

Makes enough icing for 1 dozen small gingerbread people.

Piñata Party

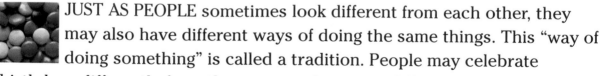

JUST AS PEOPLE sometimes look different from each other, they may also have different ways of doing the same things. This "way of doing something" is called a tradition. People may celebrate birthdays differently from the way you do, or eat different types of food, or even play different games.

One of the games children in Mexico play during their festivals (fiestas) is the piñata game. Piñatas are made of papier-mâché or light pottery. Many are shaped like animals and are filled with candy, toys, and fruit. In order to play the game, the piñata is hung above the children's heads. The children take turns hitting it with a stick while blindfolded. When it breaks, candy and toys spill to the ground.

Children in Mexico eat foods that are different than the ones you eat. Most children eat thin, round, flat bread called tortillas. These can be eaten plain or made into tacos, enchiladas, or tostadas. Frijoles (beans) that are boiled, mashed, and then fried and refried are also a traditional favorite. Many of the fruits children in Mexico eat are the same ones you eat—bananas, avocados, and mangos.

Step 1: Purchase a piñata from a large craft store or toy store. Fill it with small toys and candy.

Step 2: Before your party, prepare the ingredients to go into the tortillas: the refried beans, fiesta guacamole, grated cheese, and diced tomatoes.

Step 3: Prepare the tortillas after everyone has arrived. Let each child shape his own tortilla and pass it to an adult to cook.

Step 4: Serve tortillas, fiesta

Teachable Moments

When you talk about other cultures and traditions, note not only the differences between your culture and another one but also the similarities. Ask children the ways they think children in Mexico are different from them, and then ask them the ways in which they are alike.

guacamole, other condiments, and refried beans at your party. After dinner, play the piñata game!

Tortillas

Things you'll need:

 bowl
 spoon
 measuring cups
 measuring spoons
 wax paper
 iron skillet
warm cloth

Ingredients:

2 cups tortilla flour
1 $1/3$ cups warm water
1 teaspoon salt
$1/2$ teaspoon pepper

1. Combine all ingredients and mix well. You should have a stiff but moist dough.
2. Divide dough into ten balls and press each between sheets of wax paper until a thin, round cake is formed.
3. Heat an iron skillet and place one tortilla at a time in the middle of the skillet. Cook until brown around the edges.
4. Turn the tortilla and cook on the opposite side until puffy.
5. Wrap tortillas in a warm cloth until ready to serve.

Makes 6 to 8.

Piñata

41

Fiesta Guacamole

Things you'll need:

 knife

cutting board

 small bowl

 spoon

 measuring cup

 measuring spoons

fork

Ingredients:

1 large ripe avocado

1 tablespoon lime or
lemon juice

2 tablespoons
onion, minced

$1/4$ cup tomato,
peeled and
chopped

$1/4$ teaspoon
garlic, chopped

salt to taste

1. Cut the avocado in half lengthwise.
Pull apart the two halves.

2. Insert the point of the knife into the
middle of the pit and pull it from
the avocado.

3. Using a spoon, scrape the pulp into
a small bowl; mash the pulp with a
fork.

4. Add remaining ingredients and
blend well.

5. Fill tortillas with fiesta guacamole,
refried beans, diced tomatoes, and
grated cheese. Roll up and enjoy!

Serves 4.

Refried Beans

Things you'll need:

- saucepan
- electric mixer
- knife
- cutting board
- measuring cup
- measuring spoons
- grater

Ingredients:

1 large can pinto beans
1/2 medium onion, chopped
1/4 cup butter (1/2 stick)
3/4 teaspoon salt
1/2 cup cheddar cheese, shredded

1. In a small saucepan, heat beans to boiling.
2. Strain the liquid from the beans and mash them with an electric mixer.
3. Stir together onion, butter, salt, and beans over heat until thoroughly blended.
4. Stir in grated cheese right before removing beans from heat.
5. Fill tortillas with fiesta guacamole, refried beans, diced tomatoes, and additional grated cheese. Roll up and enjoy!

Serves 4.

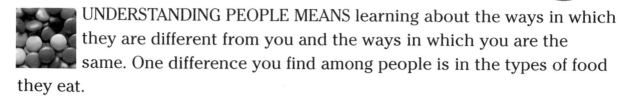

Oriental Tea Party

UNDERSTANDING PEOPLE MEANS learning about the ways in which they are different from you and the ways in which you are the same. One difference you find among people is in the types of food they eat.

People all over the world have traditional foods that they eat for many different reasons. They may have more of a certain food because it grows well in the area in which they live. Or they may eat the same types of foods their parents and grandparents ate before them. People even eat different types of foods because of their religious beliefs.

Because Americans are from many backgrounds, our food is a mixture of food traditions from all parts of the world. The hamburger was introduced in America at the 1904 St. Louis World's Fair by Germans living in St. Louis. And the fortune cookie that is so popular in Chinese restaurants today is said to have been developed by a Chinese-American in China Town (an area of San Francisco, California).

Here's an unusual party idea that will give you a chance to try something different for an afternoon snack—tea and fortune cookies! As you make this recipe and have the tea party, celebrate the fact that we are all different and we together make the world a more interesting place.

Teachable Moments

This would be a great opportunity to talk about the traditional foods your family enjoys. Explain that one reason people continue to eat the same foods the people before them ate is to continue the tradition and feel a connection to those who lived before them.

Step 1: Invite a few friends over for a tea party. If you can, find an Oriental teapot and teacups. You can prepare the flavored sugars as a group or on the day before the party.

Step 2: Make up your own "fortunes" and write them on small slips of paper to go into the fortune cookies. You may want to write them yourself or have a parent help.

Step 3: Make the fortune cookies and enjoy them with cups of Oriental tea. You may want to try several types of tea—a black tea, a green tea, or a flower tea, such as jasmine. The tea will taste best if the water is boiled for only a few minutes before the tea is added. Although this type of tea is usually served without sugar, we have included some special sugar recipes just for fun!

45

Fortune Cookies

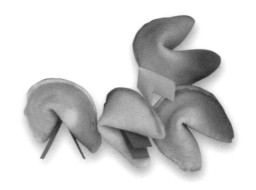

Things you'll need:

 large bowl

 wooden spoon

 measuring cups

 measuring spoons

 cookie sheet

Ingredients:

$3/4$ cup unbeaten egg whites

1 $2/3$ cups sugar

$1/4$ teaspoon salt

1 cup butter, melted

1 cup all-purpose flour

$1/2$ teaspoon vanilla extract

$1/2$ teaspoon almond extract

1. Preheat oven to 350 degrees.

2. Combine egg whites, sugar, and salt. Mix together until sugar and salt are dissolved.

3. Add butter, flour, and extracts. Stir until well blended.

4. Drop the dough by tablespoonfuls several inches apart onto a well greased cookie sheet.

5. Bake about ten minutes or until the edges are light brown.

6. Mold warm cookie over wooden spoon handle to form a cylinder. Insert "fortunes." Pinch ends together to shape the traditional fortune cookie.

Makes 2 dozen cookies.

Flavored Colored Sugars

Things you'll need:

 medium bowl
 spoon
 measuring cup
 measuring spoons

Strawberry Sugar

Ingredients:

1 cup granulated sugar
1/4 teaspoon strawberry extract
1/2 teaspoon powdered red food
   coloring

Lemon Sugar

Ingredients:

1 cup granulated sugar
1 teaspoon lemon rind, finely
   grated
1/2 teaspoon powdered yellow food
   coloring

Mint Sugar

Ingredients:

1 cup granulated sugar
1/4 teaspoon mint extract
1/2 teaspoon powdered green food
   coloring

For each flavored sugar:

1. Place all ingredients in a medium
bowl and stir thoroughly to
combine.
2. Serve as desired with Oriental tea.

Each recipe makes 1 cup.

"Happy Hanukkah" Party

RESPECT FOR OTHER PEOPLE begins with understanding them. Some of your friends may have beliefs that are different from yours. They may celebrate holidays in a different way, or they may even observe holidays you do not observe.

You don't have to believe what someone else believes to show respect. You just need to understand that they have a right to their beliefs. And even if you don't observe the same holidays and traditions, you can still have fun learning about them. One holiday some people in our country celebrate is Hanukkah.

Hanukkah is the eight-day festival of lights observed by Jewish people. It is a celebration of the religious freedom of the Jews, formerly called the people of Israel. The legend of the first Hanukkah says that only one jar of oil was found to light the holy lamp in the temple for the festival. The oil should have lasted for only one day, but instead it lasted for eight!

Hanukkah is a family time for Jewish people. A candle holder with one center candle and eight candles around it (the menorah) is used for this festival. Using the center candle to light the others, the family lights one candle a night until all eight are lit. Children are given gifts on each of the eight nights of Hanukkah, often coins. Many families eat latkes (potato pancakes) with sour cream or applesauce during the Hanukkah celebration.

Celebrating different traditions can be fun. It is also a good learning experience for the whole family.

Teachable Moments

When exposing your child to a tradition from another faith, reinforce traditions from your own faith. This will not only promote respect for other people and what they believe, but it will also give your child a chance to clarify and strengthen his own faith.

Step 1: You may want to buy a menorah for the family Hanukkah party. Or, arrange eight candlesticks with one taller one in the middle. Remind your parents that the children are usually given gifts each night, often coins. Chocolate coins are available in many stores.

Step 2: Keep an eye on the calendar to see when the festival of lights begins. On the first night, use the middle candle to light one of the eight. Continue this for seven more days.

Step 3: On the final night of Hanukkah, make the traditional latkes and serve them with applesauce or sour cream.

Latkes (LOT-kuhs)

Things you'll need:

- vegetable peeler
- grater
- medium skillet
- medium bowls
- wooden spoon
- measuring cup
- measuring spoons
- knife
- cutting board
- paper towels

Ingredients:

2 cups raw potato, grated
1/2 small onion, finely chopped
1 teaspoon salt
1 tablespoon flour
1 teaspoon baking powder
1 egg, well beaten
1/4 cup canola oil

1. Wash, peel, and grate potatoes.
2. Peel and chop onion.
3. In a medium bowl, combine the potato and onion and sprinkle with salt.
4. In a separate bowl, mix flour and baking powder and add to potato mixture.
5. Beat egg and add to the potato mixture.
6. In a medium skillet, heat oil. Drop piles (two tablespoons each) of potato mixture into hot oil.
7. Press the potato piles with a spatula to flatten them.
8. Fry for two minutes on each side or until golden brown. Drain on paper towels before serving.
9. Serve with applesauce or sour cream.

Serves 6.

Homemade Applesauce

Things you'll need:

- vegetable peeler
- knife
- medium saucepan
- measuring cup
- measuring spoons
- sieve

Ingredients:

6 baking apples
1 1/4 cups water
4 tablespoons sugar
cinnamon to taste

1. Wash, peel, core, and quarter apples.
2. Put the apples in a saucepan. Add 1 1/4 cups water.
3. Cover and simmer until apples are tender.
4. Add sugar and season with cinnamon.
5. Strain applesauce through a sieve.

Serves 6.

Just as it's important to respect all people, it's also important to appreciate and respect God's creation. Appreciating creation means realizing how special and beautiful the world is and caring about what happens to it. It means realizing that what you do has an effect on the world around you.

Appreciation for Creation

People use the earth for many things. We use food, water, energy, and other treasures from our planet. Some of these things we need to live. And some of the earth's gifts just make our lives better, easier, and more fun.

Using these natural resources, or gifts from the earth, is a good thing. That is why they are there. But if we are going to take from the earth, then we should also find ways to give back. And we must remember never to take advantage of the earth because we are selfish and want more than we need, or because we're just too busy to care. God filled the world with beautiful animals, plants, mountains, streams, and oceans. It's up to us to keep them that way, because we are the caretakers on this planet. In fact, we are the only ones who can take care of our world!

Teachable Moments

This would be a great time to focus on all the wonderful nutritious foods we get from plants in creation. Have children name some favorite fruits and vegetables and discuss how they grow—as the fruit of a plant or tree, as part of a plant (leaves or stem), or under the ground (roots or tubers). As the children better understand the important part plants play in their lives, their appreciation for creation will increase.

"Johnny Appleseed" Tree-Planting Party

Did you know you have a very valuable natural resource as close as your own yard or area park? If you have a tree close to where you live or where you play, then you have a valuable natural resource near you! You have already noticed how beautiful trees can be in the fall when their leaves turn bright reds, oranges, and yellows. But trees also provide shade and protection from the wind and sun. They are also homes for birds, animals, and insects. The roots of a tree help hold the soil in place and keep it from washing away. The leaves of a tree give us oxygen, which makes it possible for us to breathe. And trees provide us with other things, too. They give us paper, wood, and many different types of fruits and nuts. They even give us syrup! There is a legend about a young man named John Chapman who loved trees, especially apple trees. According to the legend, Johnny lived with his family on a farm in Massachusetts and loved taking care of the apple trees in their apple orchard. As wagon trains left Massachusetts on their way west, Johnny would talk about someday going west himself. His family didn't want him to leave, so they would always remind him that in the western parts of the country, there weren't any of the apple trees he loved so much. But this only made Johnny more determined. He decided to start on the long journey west and to plant apple trees along the way. So Johnny left his home in Massachusetts with a pot on his head, a Bible in his hand, and a bag of appleseeds over his shoulder. The legend says that Johnny planted apple trees all across America. He became well known and loved everywhere he went and was called by a new name—Johnny Appleseed! Here's a party idea that will give you a chance to do something good for the earth and have a party at the same time—*have a tree-planting party.* Make these delicious decorated apples after you plant your tree, and remember to eat several fresh apples every week for a nutritious, healthy snack!

Step 1: Before you plan your tree-planting party, call a local tree nursery to find out the best time of year for planting trees in your area. Even if it's not a good time to plant a tree, you can still have a party. Just plan on planting seeds in pots and growing them indoors until it's time to plant the trees outside.

Step 2: You can make neat party invitations by placing tree leaves under a sheet of paper and rubbing over the paper with the flat edge of a crayon. Use recycled paper, or recycle your own paper by using the back of paper already used in an office or a business.

Step 3: Growing a tree from seed can take a long time, so if possible, take the whole party to visit your local nursery and purchase a small tree there. Call ahead before you go, and they can probably arrange for an expert to talk to the group about trees. Ask about the best type of trees to grow in your area and the best ways to care for them.

Step 4: Ask a parent to help in finding a good location for your tree, and let everyone help with the planting. Your parent may need to start the hole for the tree. You can all help with widening the hole, putting the tree in place, adding soil, and watering.

Step 5: After you plant the tree, you'll be ready to make these delicious chocolate apples. While you work, either read or tell the story of Johnny Appleseed and his love for planting apple trees.

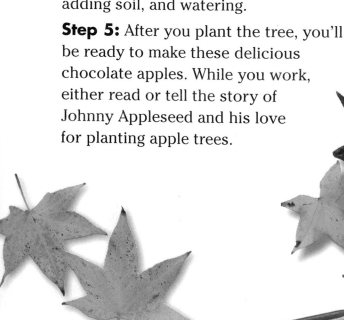

"Mr. Cat" Chocolate Apple

Things you'll need:

 wax paper

 measuring cup

 microwave-safe bowl

 wooden stick

spoon

Ingredients:

1 large apple
1 cup dark chocolate morsels
1 package colored candies
1 small package thin red licorice

1. Clean apple and place on a sheet of wax paper.
2. Place dark chocolate morsels in a microwave-safe bowl. Microwave on medium power in 40-second intervals, stirring between intervals, until the chocolate is thoroughly melted.
3. Insert the wooden stick into the center of the apple at the stem end.
4. Spoon melted chocolate onto the apple to coat thoroughly.
5. Place candies in the proper places for eyebrows, eyes, nose, and mouth.
6. Cut red licorice into one-inch pieces and place beside the nose for whiskers. If you have any trouble getting the whiskers to stick, try using tube icing as glue.

Serves 1.

55

Striped Chocolate Apple

Things you'll need:

 wax paper

 microwave-safe bowls

 measuring cup

 wooden stick

 spoon

 2 squirt bottles

Ingredients:

1 large apple
$1/2$ cup dark chocolate morsels
$1/2$ cup white chocolate morsels

1. Clean apple and place on a sheet of wax paper.

2. Place dark chocolate morsels in a microwave-safe bowl. Microwave on medium power in 40-second intervals, stirring between intervals, until chocolate is thoroughly melted.

3. Spoon melted dark chocolate into a plastic squirt bottle and place the lid on tightly.

4. Insert the wooden stick into the center of the apple at the stem end.

5. Squirt dark chocolate in up-and-down lines on the sides of the apple. Let dry.

6. Repeat the same process with the white chocolate.

Serves 1.

Sprinkled Apple

Things you'll need:

 wax paper

measuring cup

microwave-safe bowl

wooden stick

spoon

Ingredients:

1 large apple

1 cup white chocolate morsels

$1/2$ cup sprinkles, or more
   depending on size of apple

1. Clean apple and place on a sheet of wax paper.

2. Place white chocolate morsels in a microwave-safe bowl. Microwave on medium power in 40-second intervals, stirring between intervals, until chocolate is thoroughly melted.

3. Insert the wooden stick into the center of the apple at the stem end.

4. Spoon melted chocolate onto the apple to coat thoroughly.

5. Gently press sprinkles into the chocolate until the apple is thoroughly coated.

Serves 1.

Recycling Party

RESPECTING THE EARTH means taking care of it and caring about what happens to our planet. When God created the world, He placed men and women in it and told them to take care of it. But some people haven't cared about taking care of the world, and the world has suffered. Now, many people are understanding that we have created environmental problems because of our thoughtlessness and selfishness. One of these problems is too much garbage.

Some people make more trash than others, but we all make some. Often we toss everything into the same can, mix it all up together, and throw it into garbage dumps or bury it in pits. This is wasteful, because much of what we throw away in our garbage can be used again, or recycled.

Recycling is really not as complicated as it sounds. It simply means sorting your trash so that many of the things in it can be used again. Glass, paper, many things made out of metal, and some plastics can be recycled. Many areas have recycling programs in which the items to be recycled are picked up alongside the trash. In other communities, recycling centers are located near large grocery stores. Recycling can be easy when you get in the habit!

Here's a recycling party idea that will not only be fun, but will remind everyone about the importance of recycling.

Teachable Moments

Today's children seem to be more conscientious about recycling than are their parents. The enthusiasm is there; they just need to learn practical ways to avoid waste and to recycle resources. Provide them with opportunities to recycle at home, and teach them "good earth" habits while they are interested. These good habits will last a lifetime.

Step 1: Make these cute recycling invitations on grocery sacks. Ask your guests to bring the sacks to the party filled with paper or cans. (Glass bottles may break.)

Step 2: List one or two ingredients on the invitation that each person can bring to make the edible "trash" recipes.

Step 3: As your guests arrive, have them sort their trash and turn in their sacks for "clean earth dollars." Set up a "store" where the children can spend their clean earth dollars on gum, stickers, or other party favors.

Step 4: Collect all the ingredients for making the "trash." Divide into three groups and have each group make one type of trash. Eat and enjoy!

You're Invited!

To:

When:

Where:

Please bring _____

And cans/newspaper!

Main Course Trash

Things you'll need:

 large bowl

 knife

 cutting board

 measuring cups

Ingredients:

1 cup hard cheese, cubed*
1 cup peanuts
1 cup smoked turkey, cubed*
1/2 cup sunflower seeds

1. In a large bowl, combine all ingredients.
2. Stir thoroughly until well mixed.

Serves 6 to 8.

*Miniature cookie cutters may be used to cut the turkey or cheese into shapes, if desired.

Healthy Trash

Things you'll need:

 large bowl

 knife

cutting board

 measuring cup

Ingredients:

1 cup carrots, sliced*
1 cup celery, sliced*
1 cup jicama, cubed*
1 cup red pepper, cubed*
1 cup raisins

1. In a large bowl, combine all ingredients.
2. Stir thoroughly until well mixed.

Serves 6 to 8.

*Miniature cookie cutters may be used to cut the vegetables into shapes, if desired.

Dessert Trash

Things you'll need:

 large bowl

measuring cup

Ingredients:

- 1 cup plain chocolate candies
- 1 cup chocolate covered peanut candies
- 1 cup white chocolate morsels
- 1 cup gummy bears
- 1 cup malted milk balls

1. In a large bowl, combine all ingredients.

2. Stir thoroughly until well mixed.

Serves 6 to 8.

61

Zoo Party

IT IS IMPORTANT for us to remember to take care of our world, because we do not live here alone. We share the earth with other creatures. And because we don't live on our planet alone, our actions affect not only other people, but all the different types of birds, animals, insects, and other wildlife in the world. The tiniest ant and the largest whale are affected by the way we treat our world.

One of the best ways to remind ourselves of the beauty and specialness of all God's creation is a trip to the zoo. Not only will it be fun to visit all the animals, but it will also be a reminder of the incredible variety found in creation.

Step 1: Invite a few friends and their parents to take a trip with you to the zoo, with lunch as your treat. Have everyone bring a backpack. Prepare the animal crackers and monkey chow the night before. Prepare the sandwiches in the morning.

Step 2: Freeze boxed drinks ("Jungle Juice") and wrap each lunch separately for each person to carry in his backpack. The frozen drink should keep the food at a safe temperature.

Teachable Moments

During this trip to the zoo, familiarize the children with the words *extinct* and *endangered*. Emphasize the special qualities of each species, and talk about our responsibility in taking care of all the incredible creatures God created to live in our world.

Backpack Bundle Sandwiches

Monkey Face Sandwiches

Things you'll need:

 knife

cutting board

 measuring cups

Ingredients:

4 slices wheat bread
4 slices favorite dark brown bread
1/2 cup peanut butter
1 large banana, sliced
1/4 cup currants
8 large marshmallows
8 raisins or chocolate morsels
chocolate tube icing

1. Place the wheat bread on the cutting board and cut a fat "eight" shape from each slice for the monkey faces.
2. Place the dark brown bread on cutting board and cut a circle shape with ears from each slice for the monkey heads.
3. Spread the "eight" shapes with peanut butter, top with banana slices, and sprinkle with currants. Cover with dark brown bread and turn the sandwiches over.
4. Decorate outside of monkey faces with marshmallows and raisins (or chocolate morsels) for eyes and chocolate icing for mouth.

Serves 4.

Elephant-Shaped Tortilla Sandwiches

Things you'll need:

 elephant-shaped cookie cutter (or paper pattern)

 knife

cutting board

 measuring spoons

Ingredients:

8 large flour tortillas
4 slices American cheese
4 tablespoons apple chutney

1. Place each tortilla on the cutting board and cut with an elephant-shaped cookie cutter (or cut around a paper elephant pattern).
2. Place each slice of American cheese on the cutting board and cut with the elephant-shaped cookie cutter or paper pattern.
3. Spread one side of each tortilla with 1/2 tablespoon chutney.
4. Place cheese slice on one tortilla and top with a second tortilla to make four sandwiches.

Serves 4.

Monkey Chow

Things you'll need:

 measuring cup

large plastic bag

Ingredients:

1 cup banana chips
1 cup dried apricots
1 cup dried pineapple
1 cup dried papaya

1. Pour all ingredients into a large plastic bag.

2. Shake to combine.

Serves 4.

Chocolate-Dipped Animal Crackers

Things you'll need:

- microwave-safe container
- measuring cup
- measuring spoons
- spoon
- wax paper

Ingredients:

1 cup chocolate morsels
1 tablespoon whipping cream
1/2 teaspoon vanilla extract
24 animal crackers
sprinkles

1. In a microwave-safe container, place chocolate morsels, cream, and vanilla extract.
2. Microwave on medium power in 40-second intervals, stirring between intervals, until the chocolate morsels are melted.
3. Cover the counter with wax paper.
4. Dip half of each animal cracker into the melted chocolate and then into sprinkles, leaving half of each cracker uncoated.
5. Place on wax paper to dry.

Serves 12.

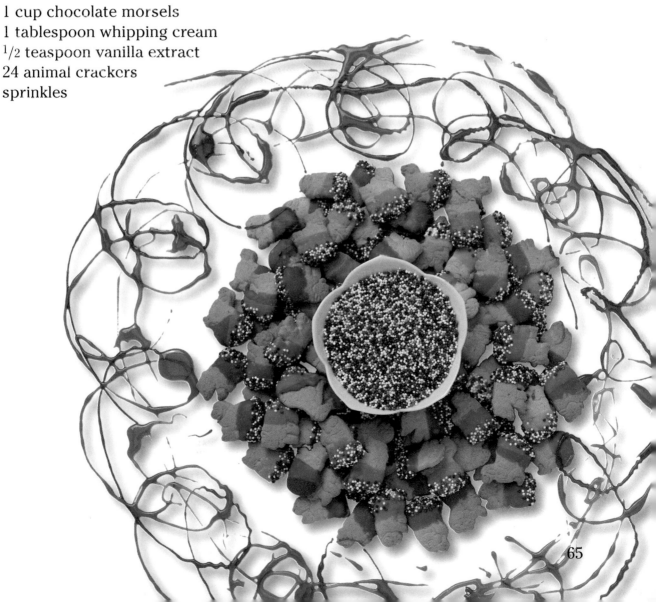

Family Clean-Up Party

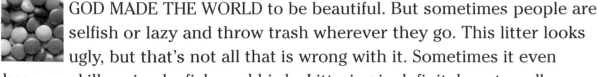

GOD MADE THE WORLD to be beautiful. But sometimes people are selfish or lazy and throw trash wherever they go. This litter looks ugly, but that's not all that is wrong with it. Sometimes it even harms or kills animals, fish, and birds. Littering is definitely not cool!

There may not be much you can do to clean up all the oil spills in Alaska, or to pick up cans on the beautiful beaches in Hawaii, but you can clean up areas around you. You may want to start with your own yard, and then you can move to an area park. Or you may even want to have a clean-up time on your next family camping trip.

Wherever you decide to clean up, you will need something to put the litter in. A cereal box with the top cut off and a cord tied for a handle works nicely. You can wear this over your shoulder so your hands will be free to pick up the litter. You may want to make each person in the family responsible for one type of trash. Then it will already be sorted for recycling.

After the work is done, make these fun banana splits. If you are camping, you can cook them over a campfire. If you are in a park or in your own back yard, a barbecue grill will work great, too.

Teachable Moments

Even one short afternoon picking up litter can have an effect on a child for years to come. After he's spent a few hours picking up trash, he will not be likely to throw any down in the future. He will have learned valuable lessons about the importance of self-control, consideration for others, and respect for God's creation. Make the day fun by giving prizes for the most trash collected.

Cookout Banana Splits

Things you'll need:

 knife

measuring cups

foil

Ingredients:

4 to 6 bananas
$1/2$ cup peanut butter
$1/2$ cup mini marshmallows
$1/2$ cup mini chocolate morsels
maraschino cherries

1. Peel the bananas and slice them most of the way lengthwise, leaving the bottom of the banana attached.
2. Spread the insides of the banana with peanut butter.
3. Sprinkle with mini marshmallows and mini chocolate morsels.
4. Wrap each banana in aluminum foil and place it on the fire or grill until the marshmallows and chocolate melt.
5. Arrange grilled bananas on a plate and top with maraschino cherries.

Serves 4.

All people in the world have needs. A person may need something for her body, such as food, clothes, or protection from the rain and cold. She may need something for the inside, such as someone to talk to when she is lonely or a hug from someone when she is sad.

Serving Others

People also have wants—things they wish for but could survive without. Some people may wish for their own home, or books for school, or a few toys. Most of us have enough of everything we need. We have food to eat, clothes to wear, and a roof over our heads. We have people who love us and friends to keep us company. Many of us even have much of what we want. We have many different outfits to wear to school, books to read, and so many toys that we have a hard time fitting them all into our closets. But there are people who don't have everything they need or much of what they want. They may be hungry, or homeless, or lonely and sad. They may not have enough money for extra clothes, coats, books, or toys. If you have been blessed with enough clothes, plenty of food, and a home, then it's important for you to help others who don't have as much. Helping others who need help is called service. And serving others is one of the most important parts of life. There are many ways of helping others. People all around you are lonely, sad, or hungry. Sometimes we don't help other people because we don't know how. Sometimes we may need to be reminded that we need to. This section contains some party ideas that will give you and your friends and family a chance to do something for others. Making these recipes should be great fun, and the good feeling you will have because you did something nice for another person will be even better. But the best part of all will be knowing you did what was right in the eyes of God.

Food Bank Party

 HELPING PEOPLE DURING THE HOLIDAYS is great, but there are also agencies that help people all through the year. Your local food bank is one of these places. Food banks are a source of food for many people who would otherwise not have enough to eat.

Many families would be glad to contribute to their local food banks, but it is often inconvenient to do so. This party idea will give several families a chance to give to others. And as a special treat for everyone who helps, make these colorful Lollipop Cookies.

Step 1: Before you have your party, look in your telephone directory to find a food bank near you. Many of them are listed under Community Service Organizations or Helpful Numbers. Call a local food bank to find out what types of food donations they need and where and when you can deliver them.

Step 2: Invite several friends over to do a fun cooking activity and to take a donation of food to a local food bank. Ask each person to bring two or three items to donate to the food bank. Peanut butter, canned soups, and canned meats and vegetables are good choices.

Step 3: After collecting the food for the food bank, make the lollipop cookies together. Wrap up half the cookies in colored plastic wrap, and take them to give as a special treat to the people who work at the food bank. Return to the party and enjoy the remaining cookies!

Teachable Moments

As each child arrives with her food donation, thank her for her help in feeding people who are hungry. Put the food into a big basket or box with a bow on it. Explain that the food is going to people who don't have enough to eat, people who might otherwise go hungry.

Lollipop Cookies

Things you'll need:

 wax paper

 rolling pin

 various cookie cutters

 cookie sheet

 12 six-inch wooden skewers

 cake cooling rack

spatula

Ingredients:

1 package prepared sugar cookie dough

flour

1. On a sheet of wax paper that has been sprinkled with flour, roll out the sugar cookie dough to a thickness of $1/4$" to $3/8$".
2. Use your favorite cookie cutters to cut shapes out of the dough.
3. Gently place the cookie dough shapes onto the ungreased cookie sheet. For each cookie, insert a skewer from the bottom into the center of the dough thickness and push up to the top of the cookie.
4. Bake at 375 degrees for eight to ten minutes or until lightly browned. Cool. Do not lift the cookie with the skewer until it is thoroughly cooled and iced.
5. Remove cooled cookies from cookie sheet with a spatula and place on cake cooling rack over wax paper.

Makes 2 dozen.

Fruited Sugar Icing

Things you'll need:

 bowls
 measuring cup
 measuring spoons
small pitcher
squirt bottles

Ingredients:

1¹/₂ cup powdered sugar, sifted
2 to 3 tablespoons apple juice
favorite colors of food
    coloring

1. Combine the powdered sugar and fruit juice in a medium bowl. Mix thoroughly.

2. Place the fruited icing in a small pitcher and pour over all the cookies. Let dry.

3. Pour remaining icing into separate bowls. Mix in your favorite colors. If needed, add more powdered sugar to thicken.

4. Pour one color of colored fruited icing into squirt bottle. Squirt in a back-and-forth motion over the white frosting. Be sure to let cookies dry between icing colors. Repeat the same process with each color.

Makes enough icing for 1 dozen cookies.

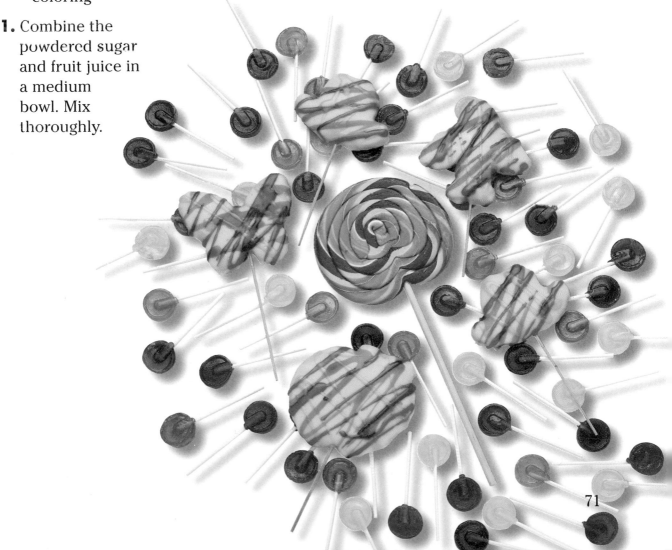

71

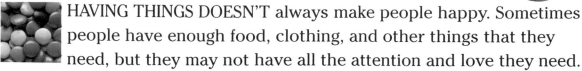

Nursing Home Party

HAVING THINGS DOESN'T always make people happy. Sometimes people have enough food, clothing, and other things that they need, but they may not have all the attention and love they need. Sometimes they are sick and can't get out and be around people. And sometimes they are just too old to do much.

Many elderly people live in nursing homes because they need a lot of care and help to live. It is too hard for them to get out and go to the doctor, to church, or even grocery shopping. They may not have much company, and they may not get to spend much time around children.

One of the best things you can do for these people is to visit them. They will love seeing a happy, smiling face! And you will get to make new friends.

People often take cookies and sweets when visiting nursing homes, but many of the people living in the home are on special diets. Instead, make cards or small gifts for the residents. After you return, make some delicious Peanut Butter and Jelly Bars for a special treat with your friends.

Step 1: Have a parent contact the social services director or activities director at a local nursing home. Find out about special needs the residents may have and plan a good time for a visit.

Step 2: Invite a few friends to visit the nursing home with you. Before you go, make pretty greeting cards to take and give to the residents.

Step 3: After your visit, return home to enjoy Peanut Butter and Jelly Bars. Talk about memorable parts of your visit.

Teachable Moments

Consider starting an adopt-a-nursing-home program in your school, church, or neighborhood. The nursing home residents will not be the only ones to benefit from this experience. Talk to the social services director about giving the residents opportunities to make small gifts for the children.

Peanut Butter and Jelly Bars

Things you'll need:

 saucepan

 measuring cups

 measuring spoons

 baking dish (8" x 8")

 large spoon

squirt bottle

Ingredients:

2 tablespoons shortening
1 cup sugar
2 eggs
1 teaspoon vanilla
    extract
3 tablespoons
    peanut butter
3/4 cup flour
1/2 teaspoon
    baking powder
1/2 teaspoon salt
1/4 cup peanuts,
    chopped
3 tablespoons
    grape jelly,
    melted

1. Preheat oven to 350 degrees.
2. In a small saucepan, melt the shortening. Remove from heat.
3. Mix in sugar, eggs, and vanilla extract.
4. Stir in all remaining ingredients except jelly.
5. Spread mixture in a greased 8" x 8" pan.
6. Using a spoon, swirl melted jelly into the peanut butter mixture.
7. Bake for 30 minutes.
8. Cool and cut into bars.
9. Optional—use a squirt bottle to squeeze melted jelly on top of each bar.

Serves 8 to 10.

"Toys for Tots" Party

 SOME TIMES OF THE YEAR are harder than others on people who are needy. Winter is harder on people who don't have coats, and Christmas is harder on children and parents who don't have extra money to buy gifts.

One program that helps provide toys for needy children at Christmas time is "Toys for Tots." "Toys for Tots" is sponsored by the United States Marine Corps Reserve. Each year, the Marines distribute pick-up boxes and posters to donation sites so people can donate new and unused toys to needy children.

Instead of the usual gift exchange, try this "Toys for Tots" party idea this Christmas!

Step 1: Have each child bring a new, unwrapped gift to the party.

Step 2: If you are having a large party, you can arrange for a representative from the Marine Corps Reserve to come in uniform to pick up the gifts. If you are having a smaller party, you may want to go as a group to one of the local drop-off sites to deliver your gifts.

Step 3: After you have given your gifts, make and eat some colorful Christmas wreath treats.

Teachable Moments

On the invitations for the party, encourage children to save their allowance or do odd jobs around the house to earn money for the gift. Their gift will mean so much more if it comes from their own efforts and resources. Children can be incredibly giving when provided with the opportunity to do so.

Mom's Christmas Wreaths

Things you'll need:

 large bowl

 double boiler

 spoon

 measuring cups

 measuring spoons

 wax paper

Ingredients:

1 stick butter
1 bag large marshmallows
2 teaspoons vanilla extract
4 teaspoons green food coloring
4 cups corn flakes
1/4 cup small cinnamon
   candies

1. Put an appropriate amount of water in the bottom of a double boiler. Place the top of the double boiler over water and heat until water boils.
2. Place butter and marshmallows in the top of the double boiler and heat until melted.
3. Remove from heat and add vanilla extract and green food coloring.
4. Put the corn flakes in a large bowl and pour marshmallow mixture over the flakes. Stir thoroughly to combine and color each flake.
5. Grease hands. Shape 1/2 cup of the cornflake mixture on wax paper to form a wreath. Sprinkle with cinnamon candies.

Serves 8.

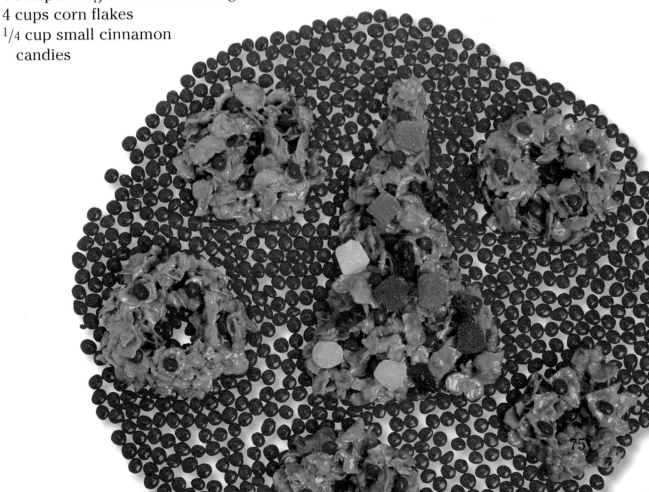

Fun Fudge Party

 SERVICE ISN'T ALWAYS DOING SOMETHING for the hungry or homeless. And service isn't always giving things. Sometimes service is doing something kind for someone, even someone in your family. Sometimes it's just paying a little bit of extra attention to someone who is lonely. One of the times when this is especially important is during the Christmas season, because Christmas can be a lonely time for many people.

If you have an older person in your family, maybe a grandparent or great-grandparent who may be feeling a little lonely during the holiday season, here's a fun fudge recipe you could make together. Just call and arrange for a special cooking time together. Or, if your family member lives too far away to visit, have a parent or older brother or sister help you make the fun fudge and take funny pictures while you cook. Send half of the fudge and the photos along with a nice card to this special person. Not only will you have spent time giving the most valuable gift of all—yourself—but you will also have some great fudge to share with the rest of your family.

Teachable Moments

Sometimes the easiest people to forget to serve are those in our own families. Even if this activity is difficult to arrange, make an extra effort to do so. Also consider making Christmas baking with Grandma or Grandpa a yearly tradition. Your child will have memories to treasure forever.

Peppermint Fudge

Things you'll need:

- medium saucepan
- spoon
- measuring cups
- measuring spoons
- square glass dish
- knife

Ingredients:

1 1/2 cups sugar
2/3 cup evaporated milk
1/2 teaspoon salt
2 cups mini marshmallows
1 1/2 cups semi-sweet chocolate
  morsels
10 peppermint candies,
  crushed
1/2 teaspoon peppermint
  extract
1 teaspoon vanilla
  extract
butter

1. In a medium saucepan, mix sugar, milk, and salt over low heat.
2. Bring to a boil and simmer for four minutes.
3. Remove from heat and add marshmallows, chocolate morsels, peppermint candies, and extracts.
4. Pour into a buttered square glass dish and refrigerate until firm. Cut into one-inch squares to serve.

Serves 10 to 12.

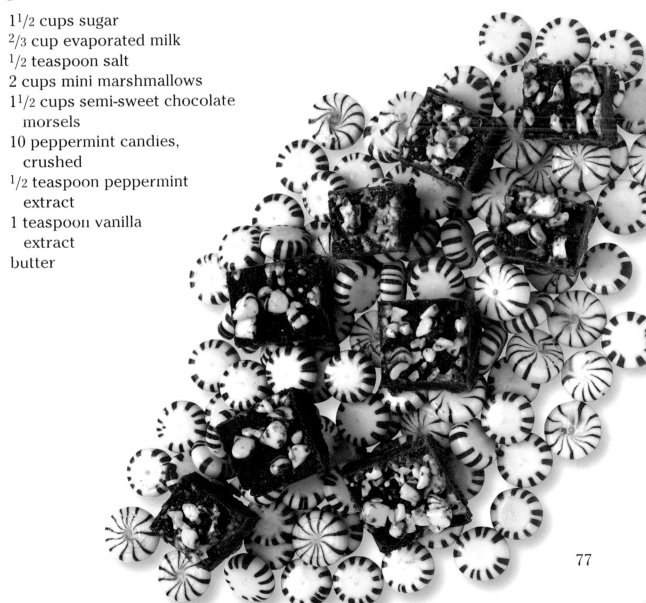

My Favorite Recipes

Party Time!

Ingredients: _____

_____

_____

_____

_____

_____

_____

_____

_____

Recipe for: _____

From: _____

Notes: _____

My Favorite Recipes

Party Time!

Ingredients: _____

_____

_____

_____

_____

_____

_____

_____

_____

_____

Recipe for: _____

From: _____

Notes: _____

My Favorite Recipes

Party Time!

Ingredients: _____

_____

_____

_____

_____

_____

_____

_____

_____

Recipe for: _____

From: _____

Notes: _____

Brief Contents

	20	Apostrophes	
	21	Semicolons	7
	22	Quotation Marks	78
	23	Other Punctuation	81
V	**Mechanics**		**87**
	24	Capitalization	90
	25	Italics	93
	26	Numbers	94
	27	Abbreviations	96
	28	Spelling	99
VI	**MultiLingual Speakers (ESL)**		**105**
	29	American Style in Writing/ESL Resources	107
	30	Verbs	109
	31	Nouns (Count and Noncount)	113
	32	Articles ("A," "An," and "The")	114
	33	Prepositions	116
	34	Omitted/Repeated Words	117
	35	Idioms	118
VII	**Research**		**121**
	36	Doing Print and Online Research	124
	37	Evaluating Print and Internet Sources	150
	38	Integrating Sources	158
	39	Designing Documents	166
VIII	**Documentation**		**173**
	40	MLA Style	176
	41	APA Style	214
	42	*Chicago Manual of Style* (CM)	235
	43	Council of Science Editors (CSE)	246
	44	Style Manuals and Resources for Various Fields	252
	Glossary of Usage		*255*
	Glossary of Grammatical Terms		*266*
	Index		*287*
	Correction Symbols		*Inside back cover*